I0156712

Salvage

Salvage

Poems by

Bruce Lowry

RAGGED SKY PRESS
PRINCETON, NEW JERSEY

Copyright © 2022 by Bruce Lowry
All rights reserved

Published by Ragged Sky Press
270 Griggs Drive, Princeton, NJ 08540
www.raggedsky.com

Library of Congress Control Number: 2022937048
ISBN: 978-1-933974-48-4

Design: Jean Foos
Photograph of author: Lynne McEniry
Cover photograph: *Salvage Barge*, Delaware River, Philadelphia,
c. 1900. Copyright A. Gurmankin.

Typefaces are Essonnes, Proxima Nova and Mercury Text G1.

Printed in the United States of America

First Edition

for my parents

Contents

I.

Where Do the Gone Things Go | 3

Salvage | 4

Boyhood, Louisiana | 5

Edge of the Delta | 6

Sitting, the Old Green Chair | 7

I Shot a Robin Once | 8

Technicolor | 9

In Trenton, My Father Turns 99 | 10

Reading Lucille Clifton to Deborah as She Plants Joe Pye Weed | 11

Leftover Fries | 12

Late Cane Sugar | 14

At a Newspaper Office, a Bottle of Ink Spills | 15

Sea Song | 16

Bayou | 17

On an August Field | 18

On Why I Became a Knicks Fan | 20

Lacrosse at Memorial Field | 21

The Day Mandela Died | 22

Rialto Theater, 1964 | 23

Honey | 24

II.

Folding the Linens | 27

Remind Me | 29

Six O'Clock on the Cape | 30

Thoughts in a Blizzard | 31

Alberta Seafood | 32

Caught in the Binary | 33

Smelling the Fruit Trees on West State | 34

Year of the Dragon | 35

Abortion Clinic, West Texas | 36

Tablets of Meaning | 37

Choice | 38

III.

Kudzu and Lime Plank | 41

You Sing Softly | 43

Iseult | 44

Alto | 46

Sunny Day in Queens | 47

Killington, in July | 49

Tears of the Locust | 50

Sitting, Staring from a Bench at the Metropolitan Museum | 51

Painting Smithson | 52

Conviction | 53

Minnieweather | 54

No One Could Remember the Smell of the Rain | 55

Dog Day Afternoon | 56

To Dance Like Anthony Quinn | 57

French Cinema | 58

Dress Shop in Manaus | 59

Acrobat | 60

IV.

New Figs | 63

Fern | 64

Plastic | 65

Notes on Progress | 66

Caught in the Binary (2) | 67

Last Log | 68

Legend of the Three Blakes | 69

Caught in the Binary (3) | 71

Christmas Eve | 72

Memorial Day, 2020 | 73

Memorial Day, 1969 | 74

Marine's Diary | 75

Haiku for Murakami | 76

Sundown, Orvieto | 77

Just Long Enough | 78

Leftover Cornbread | 79

Publication Credits | 81

In Appreciation | 83

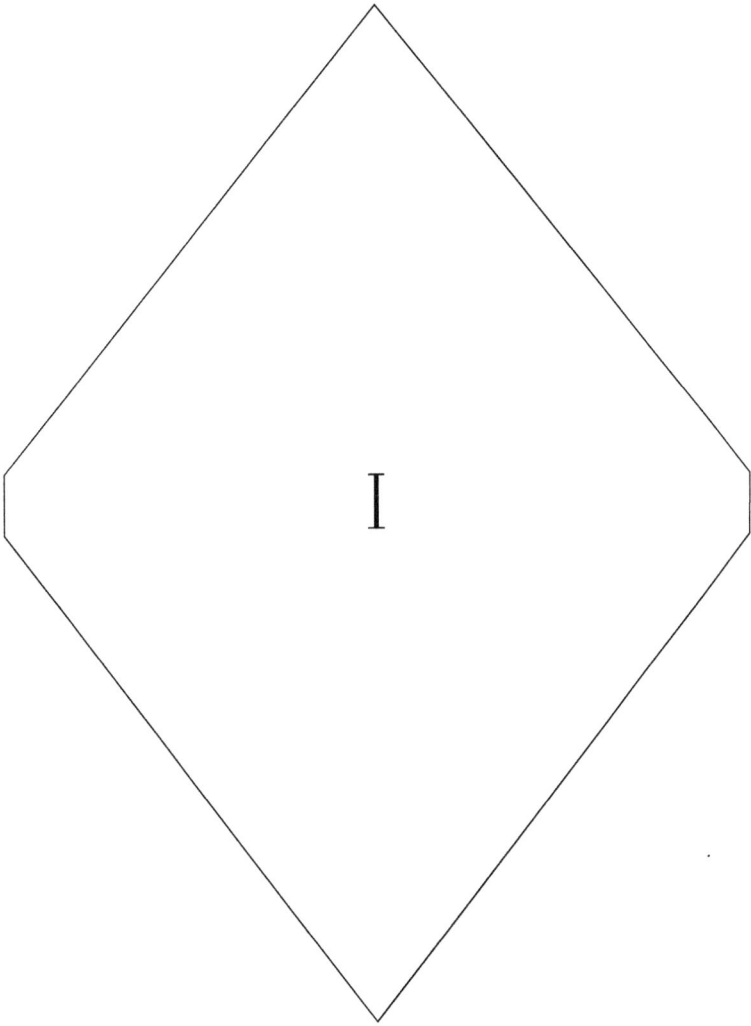

I

Where Do the Gone Things Go

from a line by Kimiko Hahn

They go into produce trucks
bound for Newark Bay,
and salt of the ocean,
loud peppermint spray.
They go into late summer
oyster beds, and bellies
of old sows, into
tiny veins of blue crab,
and the ruin of Fiterman Hall.

They burrow themselves into tops
of plum trees of my youth,
and rust of clothesline
where my mother hung
diapers on Mississippi Street,
and inside the Mason's Bible
we kept on the coffee table
but never opened,
except to add names of the dead.

Salvage

I borrowed the chicken wire
I borrowed his name
        which meant wind to me

and dawn, ponies
painted the shades of war

a salvage yard
where my father and I worked

all of one Saturday

September, naturally,
barges slugging their way up river

Boyhood, Louisiana

Mind you the tartness of cranberries soaked in a barrel
or blood from stickers on a blackberry bush
or a late gush of rain down clay hills.

Mind you the sixteen inches of Rachel's hair, the blue-
checked Pentecostal dress she'd wear,
or her mother's modest eyes.

Mind you a brother who died a swollen bird
in the bush on a foreign field, three in the afternoon
when his rifle jammed like an unleveled door.

Mind you pack animals who still remember
the soreness brought on by the cotton
and by sand and feed and gravel.

Mind you a pair of new jeans in a cedar chest,
orange spurs on the pockets, a boy who would never
wear them—but wore them once in a dream.

Edge of the Delta

Mississippi mud bank
shot glass
serpentine

Nephtalie
indeterminate age
plays Schubert

under
a mosquito net,
a red Victrola

Her dress a blue paisley
fabric cut by
her mother's good scissors

I bring her
the butter knife
for her hair

watch her fingers
pick through the dirt
and lima bean

her left foot
a dangle,
shoot vine in the air

Sitting, the Old Green Chair

Sitting, the old green chair
blinds up, floor heater
racing like a Ferrari

Here is the bourbon and here the eaves
gray sky, a tree with no leaves

Suburbs they call them, serenity
solemnity all that
crushing down of tomorrow

In the meantime, a whispering herald
chamber music, really

—the fading light
its tricks and circles, smell of coming rain
autumn foods we once cherished

fair rides we once rode
odors we gathered next to the livestock pens

our mothers daring us to taste the jams.

I Shot a Robin Once

I shot a robin once when I was eleven.
I fired the pellet, took a breath,
watched her fall from the great oak

for the very reason
I could think of none at all.

My summer would stop then as did
the familiar sounds and stale, sweet air
its tang of rust and winter

flattening in the level among the sawdust
in the wood-slatted garage

and the green fullness of the grasses.

Technicolor

We grew scallions on the east side of the house
near the clothesline—
a stone's throw away from milkweed and crepe myrtle

mixing our cultures and breath
our blood, the good blade
of the forthright

the daunting of days wearing
well your crimson jersey hung still and damp on the line
bringing out its dank September dark

and the odd late Technicolor
theories of the earth.

In Trenton, My Father Turns 99

Looking down on the groggy Delaware
—dishwater brown
and low tangle of trees—
I try to finagle my father's dreams,
what would have been his 99th birthday.

I see him drawn up with the emphysema
waffling down pave-stone streets
listening for the march of red coats
or musket fire from the Old Barracks.

I cut back away from State toward the War Memorial—

eggshells in my pocket,
mixing in the oil
and rubber of my hair,
the car seat rip, scent of turpentine in the air.

Reading Lucille Clifton to Deborah as She Plants Joe Pye Weed

I stand among women
of the grime, black
dirt on their hands
and behinds,
bending, squatting
unafraid of sweat
or hangnails caked
with blood, or
muggy August
Thursday, banging
music from
rusted shovels

Leftover Fries

It comes to me, sometimes
like the moonlight,
an end to patriot dreams,

back parking lot
at Burger City, end
of second shift.

Maura Laney and Cyndi
Oglesby stand beside my father's
blue Fairlane smoking

Marlboro Reds, loosening
their hair then their aprons,
telling me their secrets,

deciding how, exactly,
we'll divide the leftover fries,
and four pies—

three apple and a peach
fried with my own hands seven
hours ago in black grease

in the sweat of the blitz.
My shift boss, Billy Bob or
Bobby Wayne, whatever his name

was, telling me I did it
wrong except that can't be
because night air soothes

a day's labors, soaks grit
from the oven's rollers,
dares me to stare up

at the stars as I drive down
South Grand Street over
the river past midnight

and the paper mill, endless
smell of the last summer any
of us will remember—

summer of love '76 or something
like that, last one
between high school and college

between high school and the Marines
or raising babies
between what was and what

will never be again but for a time
was scandalous
and free, that fantastic moment

when all the girls were
skinny and seventeen and
the Fairlane was young and hard

and true and the bench seat
had give and my legs
had spring and Percy Sledge

was still a god. Even
the fries that fell on the floor
tasted home-made.

Late Cane Sugar

"I love that you never see Ramona with a man"—Jennifer Lopez

You attempt to define taste and the Cuban empanada—
"sweetness" you say, "it's the sweet one." Christmas parties
are made of these, faces of the sphinx, last jolt of espresso
on a Thursday morn. We pour ourselves out into newsroom
gossip like a corpse empties itself of fluid in rural Ohio
or in the late sugar cane—Ms Toston's afro—surveying
the soreness in her lungs as she recites lines from *Othello*.
"Who among us," she asks, "will breathe in leaves
of the mimosa and not be changed?" We are back there,
sophomore year in the sink with remnants of lettuce
and coffee grounds, staring at the old harbor of Santa Cruz.

At a Newspaper Office, a Bottle of Ink Spills

i hate when i bite
and taste death

red grapes beginning
their turn
in the sink

outside, a jay scuffs up his old loafers

in the snow
along the rail of the deck

it's winter, that much we know

scattering of dead leaves,
notes on the way from Edith Piaf

French sailors imagine shore leave in Algiers

my father, hair thinning, feeding
bay gulls off the ferry.

—in memory of those killed at the Charlie Hebdo
newspaper, January 7, 2015

Sea Song

I love the smell of ocean
just past two in the afternoon
when the killing-the-whale cloud is in its full glory.

I like the sound of the gulf waves, and how they remind us
somewhere down deep,
about sea songs of the ancients,

and of washbasins of old,
the scrubbing, rinsing sounds of tired hands.

Bayou

Drown me in your waters, murky
and black, that marsh where my father
baited hooks with night crawler and catalpa.

Hand me back your vaulted sky,
bream, white perch, the knob-
kneed cypress under hanging moss.

Bring back my father of those sober
Saturdays, egg salad in one hand,
my snagged line in the other,

his shoulders sagging like the long limbs
beneath the weight of things.

And bring back the last bend
where we'd lay down our poles,
paddle through the thin oak,

Coleman box of fish between us,
bait exhausted, our arms burned by the sun,
our laughter so easy then,
at home in the green and the brown.

On an August Field

Taste the tang of rubber
from a mouthpiece,
saliva and grit
and blood,
      Louisiana red clay.

"Find out if you're a man
or a mediocre,"
the line coach says,
spitting, Red Man chew
between his Rebel yells.

Third teamers we are,
the underclass, the underbelly,
the ones whose uniforms don't
fit, whose chin straps won't strap.

We could just as well have bought our
shoulder pads at the five and dime.
We are there to be stepped on
like beetles, served up
and plowed under.

Our fathers embarrassed,
our names never whispered, only
cursed in infamy when a tackle
is missed or a ball fumbled.
Our lips all bruise and crack
and burn. They will never taste
the mouth of a cheerleader or
a clean gulp of water.

Sixty years from now,
we'll relish our scars,
and rub them in reverence,

brag to our grandchildren.
"Forget wearing game jerseys
in homeroom," we'll say, "ours was
the sweet of wild onion."

On Why I Became a Knicks Fan

Because Friday nights at the Garden.
Because chaos is more fun than order.

Because Clyde Frazier, Spike Lee
        —the Knickerbockers' name.

Because Willis Reed beating
        Chamberlain on bad knees.

I think Knicks, I think four kids in the Bronx,
        beat-up asphalt, rims with no nets.
I think four kids on a Louisiana playground,
        three black, one white, no foul to be found.

I think Quon and Terry and Jimmy,
        'ballers all who

    introduced themselves with elbows
        to the chin, and jive about my pimples.

They didn't give a damn about my drunk father
        or dying sister, but sometimes
they'd feed me the ball

and sometimes I'd hit a shot.
        Quon said I was "awful"
around the basket, but "deadly" from the corner.

I see stubborn in the Knicks,
I see a scowl on Terry's face as he drains
        another jumper in my eyes.

I see the Knicks in home whites,
I see us in shirts and skins.

Lacrosse at Memorial Field

The drone of wash-and-dry
on a Saturday, while a track meet
roars past outside the east window.

Cars and buses line the street, as in
an old photo you saw once by
Walker Evans, only that one in winter

with snow on the ground, this the
first good day of spring, forsythia
peeking out like anxious fans

from the grandstand. Tomorrow
a younger set at lacrosse, with face
masks and frog-gigs, the sport

Jim Brown loved more than football—
all speed and daring, touched by hue
of science fiction. The ol' Sac and Fox,

Thorpe, he played it too, at Carlisle
before the Great War, when games were
games. We gained only from their joy.

The Day Mandela Died

Sweat beads up, shivers down my spine
like cheap cologne as a girl behind a counter
at Village Pizza, my hole-in-the-wall go to,
pushes me on the white sauce. I can't
resist her dough-powdered face in black rims,
like the glasses Mandiba wore as he
studied for the bar. Outside,
December rain comes down like hammers

pounding the gray hairs on my arms
as I try to keep the anchovy dry.
In the fog I see a tall man walking,
imagine the lepers on Robben Island
harvesting their plum fruit amid birdsong
and the late warmth of the sun.

Rialto Theater, 1964

The man in the gray
polyester slacks
makes his way
slowly up the backstairs.

I hold my father's
hand, wonder what
the word *colored* means.

The man's back is straight,
the heels
of his shoes
ride heavy on the steps.

My father leans down to me like a priest
and tells me—balcony is
a place we never go.

Honey

What you never get used to in Jersey
is the way Italian girls at the deli
call you "Honey." Back
home the best to hope
for from a great aunt at a family
reunion was "Sugar" or "Shug,"
never "Honey" or "Hon." Honey is
extra, gooey goodness. Honey
has staying power, manifestation
that the world is right, that bees are
doing what they can to save us.
The honey table is where old friends
congregate at the farmers market,
buzz around about the next bar mitzvah,
covet jars with the hive showing,
honey flowing, like it did in
Biblical times. "Honey" is sweetness
we lost in another generation
torn by war. It returns
every once in a while
in smaller, gentle doses—
the counter of our favorite
deli, on line at the Shop Rite.
It grabs onto us when we let it,
sticks to us, slows us down,
tempts us to come back for more.

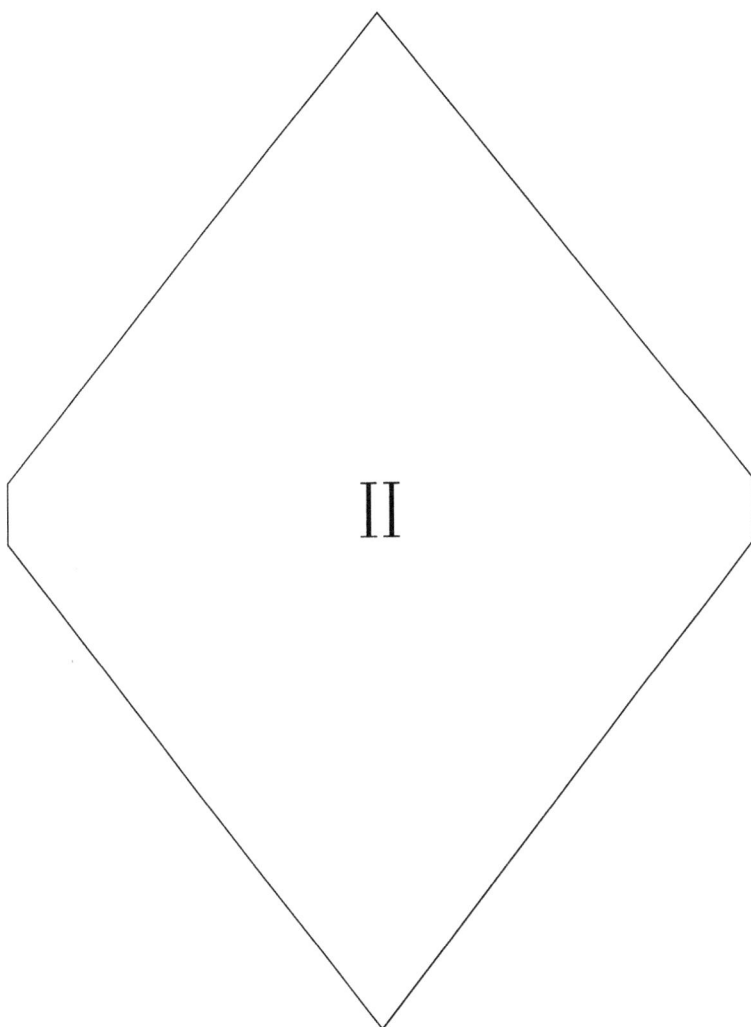

II

Folding the Linens

I went with your mother to the pavilion
in the city park where
we ran as children.

Everything was preserved,
nothing was preserved.

We flew the kites there on the Lunar
New Year, though we didn't
know what it was.

You weren't there. You were helping
your mother fold the linens.

She went to the laundromat
every Saturday, and you were there
with her to carry the old

wicker baskets and
the carton of detergent.

Girls in your eighth-grade
class thought
this funny, but it wasn't.

You helped her fold the linens
including the pink ones,

the ones with birds
that had been sewn by your sister
before she attended the Mather School of Nursing

in the autumn of '61
before she died of a hemorrhage,

a brain hemorrhage, in wine country
in the midsummer. She was twenty-two.

As for the linens, most were white
fading to yellow like lined paper in a filing cabinet

passed on by your mother's family.

You learned to fold the linens
like construction paper or Christmas wrap
—crisp and sharp at the edges.

Remind Me

Rekindle for me ancient light,
last light through the beech wood
or the red glow of the Redneck Riviera in July.

Remind me of when we were seventeen, and you came
in the candlelight, tasting of oatmeal.

Show me, if you're of a mind,
blackened fields from the drought of '21
or the mass grave along the banks of the Tennessee.

Pitch back with me, just once more
to the blue skies of Spain

or the time we lay there for hours
in the place of the Maccabees,
drawing on a rise in the flood plain for quiet breath.

Six O'Clock on the Cape

On the Cape, everything
that gets wet eventually dries:
Zoe's yellow coat,
the wings of a cormorant,
the currants
of cloud in the Western sky.

Everything gets wet,
then dries like the insides
of my mother's shoes
after her days sewing cushions
or the asphalt in the Safeway parking lot.

Somewhere to the west beyond Boston
lies the girl from geometry class
I kissed in the back of the bus
in the autumn of '71.

The rains had come, then gone
—and the dying had begun.

Thoughts in a Blizzard

after Jean Valentine's "Red Cloth"

Must be blood or birth
or both.

Must be what can't
be seen, or can.

A grease rag, maybe,
waving off a log truck,

a bandanna used on a bloody
nose in fourth grade.

Janis Joplin,
her Port Arthur days.

My mother, my sister,
my own blistered hand

pulling a red sled
through the snow.

Alberta Seafood

She would have been wearing clothes to support her legend

Something sleek and green, perhaps

She would have tasted of wildflowers from Neptune's garden

And sea spray made by a freighter under Norwegian flags

She would have fed me cod off a wooden plate; we would have

Warmed ourselves by a small fire on the beach

She would have been silent, gray hair pulled back,

A tangle of knotted fishnet, with gills intact

        —a single, orphaned eye that was black

Caught in the Binary

Caught in the terrible binary,
berries and the tree

snow flurry, and robins,
flaxseed oil, and floor wax.

In Jersey, this counts as
something approaching fabulous,

family time when faith was valid
when wind blew down Garret Mountain

and cardinal-painted lorries
hauled deli meats over to Lodi

then Wyckoff, and up to Rockland County.
I recall them in the wolf light, like the time

we ran down the summer fade
to hear the sound of the Falls.

Not see them, only listen,
imagine a rush through the channels,

space, time, ice and contemplation,
before man made claim to them

as if they were winnings at a craps table,
as if they had no say, no service

but according to his desire,
flesh, blood, free and chained

as if sound were free, and wind
as if mulch and marrow
as if scrape of arrow and skin.

Smelling the Fruit Trees on West State

Smelling the fruit trees outside
the state library is a wind song,
a chiming of the senses
clear as the clouded
glass of Coke bottle chimes
my cousin would hang
in her low yard on South Grand
Street near the curve in the river,
near the heart of things
and the dirty streams that run
through it in winter
and now the songbirds
are drunk and drowning in it—
the nectar and the only swift
moment and the sweet cream of early spring.

I stand with it another moment
hear the hard notes
my back to the Delaware
where the dinosaurs
waded with their children
an unpaid
phone bill, stamp attached
and sweating
in my bare hand.

Year of the Dragon

Child of the black prairie, I never knew this
bright holiday—lanterns, fireworks,
parades through Chinatown,
monster teeth screaming off the front
page of the *Ledger*.

See it in skittish wings of sea gulls
feasting on lo mein and leftover pizza
in a parking lot off Route 46.
"They're up from the shore,"
says an old-timer. "They come up
along the Passaic, hunting for food."

The last time I saw *Year of the Dragon*
was high school, the broken down
Rialto with a girl
from newspaper staff.

She was part Choctaw and had brown eyes.
I went with her once
to her grandfather's funeral.

He'd been a seaman in Truman's navy,
and I stood with her in the rain
and the elders stood quiet

as we sang the hymns of the whites.
Stray dogs barked in the realms
of the marsh, and later

we fed them chicken scraps from the table,
for which they seemed grateful.

Abortion Clinic, West Texas

In the waiting room I think of my mother,
her hair
when it smells of lemons.

Too many straights and squares
—a brown clipboard,
black-lined boxes, a pen
that won't write.

"No ma'am," I hear myself say
to the woman—"Never before."

The room cold, nearly empty.
Lights too bright.
All the nurses are white.

I retake my seat, notice a fleet
of ships on the wall—
an ocean more alone than real.

Tablets of Meaning

Orange Kubota—long black claw—impersonates T-Rex
or a saber-tooth tiger picking bones of the old Texaco—
exposing veins, organs, splattering guts of the pumps
recalling fossils from whence they came that time
when Earth stood there winking at the minor prophets,
their tablets of meaning, stood there by the freeway
shouting like Amos with his hair on fire in rush hour
in a place where ponies once wore
colors of the tribes and ran for their supper.

Choice

If given a choice
I'll walk the grass
over graves of twelve parakeets
instead of blue concrete.

I'll reach for black salve
in my mother's medicine cabinet
on the lower shelf
next to the Castor oil.

If given a choice
I'll take the 78 bus to Linden
through Elizabeth
to sit by the pockmark-faced girl

who cleans floors in a pharmaceutical
lab and munches Zero bars
on her lunch break.

She must be a fabulist, I think
who conquers the silences
who floats on the oily rivers they provide.

If I have a choice
I'll remember my mother in her
work clothes
with her Sanka
and cigarettes

bent towards the kitchen window
before she heads out the door
into dark morning
into the old hand of day.

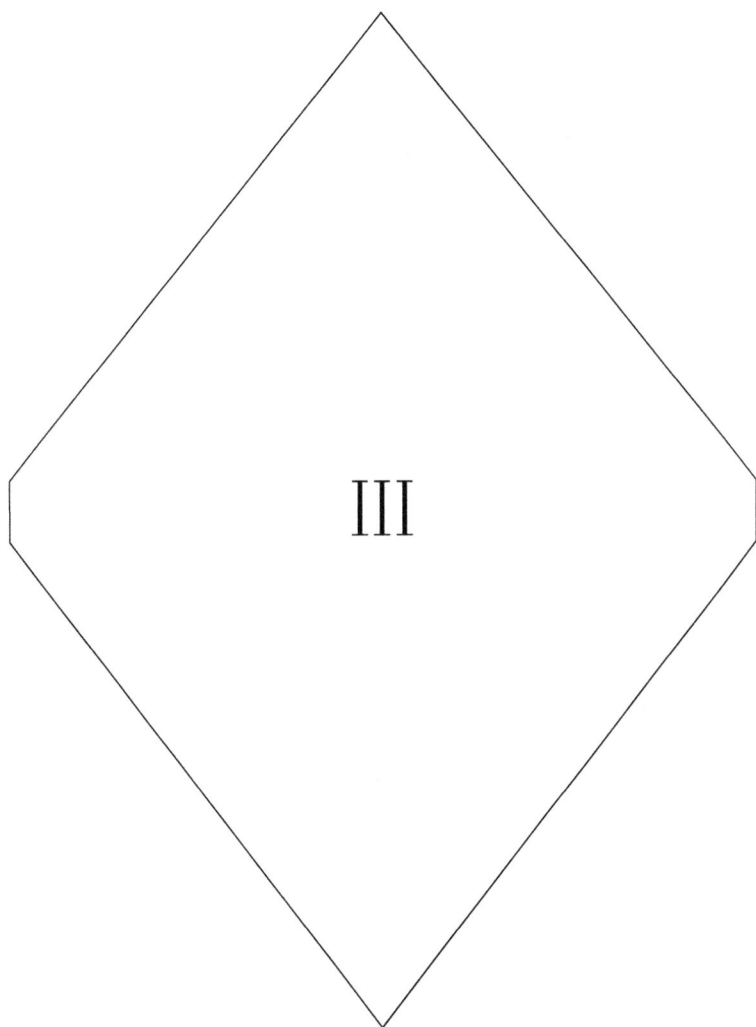

III

Kudzu and Lime Plank

I'm eating pork chops at Norman's, my father's
favorite restaurant, fantasizing

about my therapist in Jersey, whose hair
is gold, crinkly as curly Qs

we used to scarf down on football
Friday nights in the South.

It drives me crazy, her hair, sexy
steamy like crazy Glenn Close in that movie.

I'm staring straight at her when she tells
me I'm her first, Southerner that is, the

tormented kind, the Capote-Percy-Tennessee
Williams kind, the kind

who might throw himself in the Charles
River like Quentin Compson kind.

A man who will search three hours for
Louis Armstrong's headstone

or pour whiskey on Faulkner's grave.
She wants to know why I carry

it, the guilt, and yet still marvel
at gallantry and Pickett's Charge.

It's complicated, I hear myself say.
There's something in the soil,

in kudzu and lime plank, in lichen
and worm and metal and blood.

You can't wash it away with law or virtue,
or words, or cleanse desire from the hollers.

It's under the nails. Scrape at if you like,
see if the dirt changes color.

You Sing Softly

for Alan, from a line by Chris Abani

You sing softly to him in a language
from the Magyars, or Carthaginians
peoples who have come through
wars and the child's blood of wars.

You sing softly in a language
of snowflake and stone
forgoing lullaby in the name
of sustenance and economy.

You sing softly in a language
according to a flock of migrating
workers headed east, the same language
Bashō spoke in service of the tulip.

You sing to him a language
he will never understand,
language of dirt on the hand
and sweat on the brow.

You sing finally a song from the Psalter,
kneel onto a prayer rug pointing
toward Mecca. You find your brother
there—a soothsayer, or a Spartan—
then start again home.

Iseult

The day
Iseult
Gonne
first cast
her spell
on Yeats
she must have
held the scent
of Burberry
or my kitchen
in August
fresh cut
daisies
pink, purple
and white
mixed w/
old garlic
stewing
new shrimp
or maybe
outside
in late
grass and
earthworms
come up
to be eaten
by robins
or like
Bushmills
in a brown
glass or
by grace, maybe

her smell
was nothing
more than
youth
which to men
like Yeats
men like me
is by then,
but one more
word for death.

Alto

don't mind the cat gut on the window
or yellow jackets
making hay
in the barn

my Uncle Louie
no-hit the Alto Red Caps
on two days' rest

on a winter
Sunday
in July

before picking season

tobacco juice rolled down
his lip drawing the green flies

Sunny Day in Queens

We've hit on a tiny antique store in Astoria,
    and damned if an 8-track player
        isn't squeezing out

the pure honey, Hank Williams
    singin' "Honky Tonk Blues."
        I want to grab the shop owner,

who looks to be in her 70s,
    and do the Texas two-step
        next to the edge of her finest

china. I want to shake her, speak
    her language, tell her nobody can keep
        still listening to this music.

I want to regale her with stories how
    my father, so drunk he could barely stand,
        would grab my mother on

Saturdays, listening to the Opry
    and cut a rug across the old
        wood floors of our living room.

I want to engage this woman about music
    and relic, the machine my sister's
        boyfriend would play

all his Johnny Rivers and Jerry Lee Lewis
    records on when waters were low
        behind the levees

and he'd take me along, top down
    as we cruised South Monroe in
        a '67 cinnamon-red GTO.

I want to do all this before Hank hits
     the last honeyed note and dies
         in the back seat of a '52 Cadillac

leaving me stranded there in a foreign field,
     so nearly perfect, so sunny I can hardly see.

Killington, in July

Among the redwood cottages the wind
blows down the green mountains

as if howling in from the sea.
I swear I hear a foghorn follow

bellowing from the throat of a Norseman
though there is no fog—

only the crisp white of late
sunlight like the collar of a groomsman.

      *

Somewhere there is a wedding
cake with my name on it

written in old Welsh, among back trails
where run the rabbits and hounds

and particulars of the twilight
we cherished once

inside a country church, stained glass
ringing in our ears with the blood

      *

and the power of the blood we held
so fast in the Broadman Hymnal—

where the black letters clung
to the pages, and the pages

had begun
to yellow against the white.

Tears of the Locust

Beginning to be drenched by all the crying
long black pea pods

my grandmother's black veil
entwined in a rosary—

three lost lovers
small oak leaves stuck to tires of an old Prius

parked under a purple haze
mingling with the rutted asphalt of the living.

Sitting, Staring from a Bench at the Metropolitan Museum

I want Pollock to paint
my face with all its pocks and crags—
all its glory
all its canyon roads and rocky hills.

I want Pollock to lay it out
on the floor and stomp it to bits
like a schoolyard bully in seventh grade
then heal it up with ink,

thread and black salve
the way Sister Roye did that day
in chemistry lab, stretching
blue veins in her fingers

holding another child together with glue.

Painting Smithson

In 1962 Alice Neel painted Robert Smithson blemishes and all
the way I would if I could hold a brush.

Like the Kintsugi mending pottery with lacquer and gold
showing the cracks, accenting them in fact

making them part of the whole.
As she explained in the museum catalogue

she wanted to show "Smithson's acne-stricken face"
—its ugliness, modesty, its beauty

the way the artist himself must have imagined his work,
Partially Buried Woodshed,

in Ohio—the eaves, the latticework, the dirt
raw beauty, damage entering decline

earth mixing with iron, age and corruption
—red rust and peel and rain.

Conviction

Unsure of anything, most of all myself, I order edamame.

While the waiter stands in her black hair and vest and Santa's cap
I practice pronouncing—*eda—ma-me, eda—ma-me.*

Under my breath then aloud, *eda—ma-me*
as she pours water over electronica and shattered glass.

"I'll have that out, in a second," she says with a smile
and only the hint of conviction.

This world we know: "edamame" implies conviction
—the slow peel, the tongue and the salt.

"In a second," does not.

Conviction is sticky business—grease in a barrel
the Second Thermidor or red beret—that game
we played with hexagonal glass windows in third grade.

The way a fire ant will attack
one last hill at sunset.

Or the time and care my student takes to braid her deskmate's
hair instead of completing her essay on Cheever.

When the edamame arrives, I think of the Japanese—
their greens and poets, their flowers,
potteries of occupation.

I ask myself why we try so hard to obliterate words with deeds.

Minnieweather

I never noticed before the paint-store
windows on River Road

how the odd-shaped brick staggers
so terribly against the adobe.

How it spells out yellow then off-white
colonial, bringing to mind

Ol' Minnieweather, my art teacher
in seventh grade, first time

we were all together then in our
separate colors and hair,

sporting combs, drawing
green apples, blue candles, white tracing paper,

Minnieweather ever watching,
himself almost a painting:

coffee-burned arms exaggerated
under short pastel sleeves

like soil up from the Delta my father
swallowed as he grew strong

sharecropping alongside Black men
and Mexican, all of them

making art with the clay
given, investigating never-ending

daylight in shades of orange and gray,
fingers navigating landscapes

like those we brought to life
with our crayons or the stilled water

we used to clean our brushes.

No One Could Remember the Smell of the Rain

from a line by Sally Ashton

Or corn tortillas as we came down fast
detoured away from the fires.

Winds were water for our eyes,
the only map a crummy one

from a hotel in Santa Barbara
with pink stucco peeling

off the walls near a portico.
We did not ask for disaster

only peace, tales
indigo in the tattooed streaks

along the forearms of a tall woman
with braided, silver hair

who said she'd bought
her conch shell for a necklace

"at a thrift store in Ventura."

In those days, we longed to go places
that sapped our energy and starved our souls

even in November
among the white ash of wildfires

that give off a soft, yellow streak
from a lost millennium—

our reflections of time in one with Milton
rolling out with the tides

and the dog gods of the sea.

Dog Day Afternoon

Emil Jannings, probably a Nazi,
won the first best
actor Oscar in 1929 for playing
an exiled Russian general in *The Last Command*.

Another actor, Lionel Pina,
played "Pizza Boy"
in *Dog Day Afternoon*.

When we quarantine
we miss the wide screens
and popcorn popping out names
inside a machine.

In 2007 I saw Heath Ledger play Robbie Clark
in *I'm Not There*.

This was at the Film Forum
on a fall day when a million people were bunched
together in the hurry
of afternoon, and hurried the sundown
past the waterfront
wearing their first goose-down jackets of the season.

I walked among them out of the theater
rubbing my hands in the dying light.

To Dance Like Anthony Quinn

I've always wanted to walk through Athens in the rain.

Listen to the laughter of the old Greeks.
Take a swig of the good stuff.

I've always wanted the skinny legs of a dancer,
to dance like Anthony Quinn.

Yesterday on the train from Portland
a young woman with
hiking gear and trekking poles
said she'd walked
five hundred miles up
the West Coast
in the rain and wind.

Her legs were the size of a wren's.

Exiting in Seattle, she was a ghost
gone so soon I wondered
whether she'd been
there at all—so soon is our life on trains
—ferries we hardly remember them.

Or the spray of the ocean.
Or the look on our faces tasting the salt of it.

French Cinema

Reading the *Times'* review of Tavernier's new film,
a documentary on French cinema,

I could not recall which you liked best,
the French or the Italians,

couldn't help but think what it might
have been like in the spring of '82

to go to the movies with you,
some place down in the Village,

Jules et Jim, say, or *The Bicycle Thief*,
and after to dissect them in a small café,

with espresso and cigarettes
as if we were old lovers,

to see your face clench in frown
then unroll in a joy of light

so that it covered the table
like a pale linen cloth

from a black-and-white film,
Bergman maybe

or one of the Japanese,
a picture crowds had flocked

to see many times before,
and would gladly see again.

Dress Shop in Manaus

Her head turn is the Samba, an entire
culture in a mirror, the dress close
to her chest, a partner to be pushed away

like a bother, like the rains outside, afternoon-
long, unforgiving rain of the Amazon.

"You like this one," she declares more
than asks. Its sleek blackness is the ticket
holding the supple lines of her form.

Like the hotel, the shop is white-wash
colonial, out of Kipling or Maugham,
stocking only the best cuts of the season.

She comes close now, drowning you,
a déjà vu of rainwater and hair. Later,
at the old Opera House, she will wear it up,

remind you of Claudia Cardinale in the havoc
of the opening scene of *Fitzcarraldo*

and you will do what mad men like Kinski
have done through the ages,
stand there, paralyzed

by the darkness of her beauty—
by her wrists, by her red vest and black shawl,
by her long dancer's legs.
You would slit your wrists for the combs in her hair.

In the intermission she will ask for water
and you will fetch it, and as you hold
it out, you will swallow hard,
taste your own salt, feel
the last parts of the soul bleed out.

Acrobat

I once made love to an armless vet
who said she was from Cleveland, but was not.
She was from L.A.
The blue piping
descending from her shoulders
glowed in the night
like the old ink lamps
my father worked under in the '60s
at Twin City Printing
when his eyes were bad
and the Vietnam War
was going that way.

She was an acrobat, she told me,
before the war
"like Burt Lancaster."
"He was my mother's favorite," I said.

We drank licorice tea, our legs akimbo
and I noticed for the first time burn scars
starting at her ankles then leaping up
her legs like wildfire.
She wasn't even in combat
when it happened, she said,
but on something called "body sweep."

I never saw her after that,
and to be honest, was not
sure I wanted to. What I did
do was devour the green grapes and Syrian
bread she'd left behind on the counter
next to the dates and her
number printed in blue script.

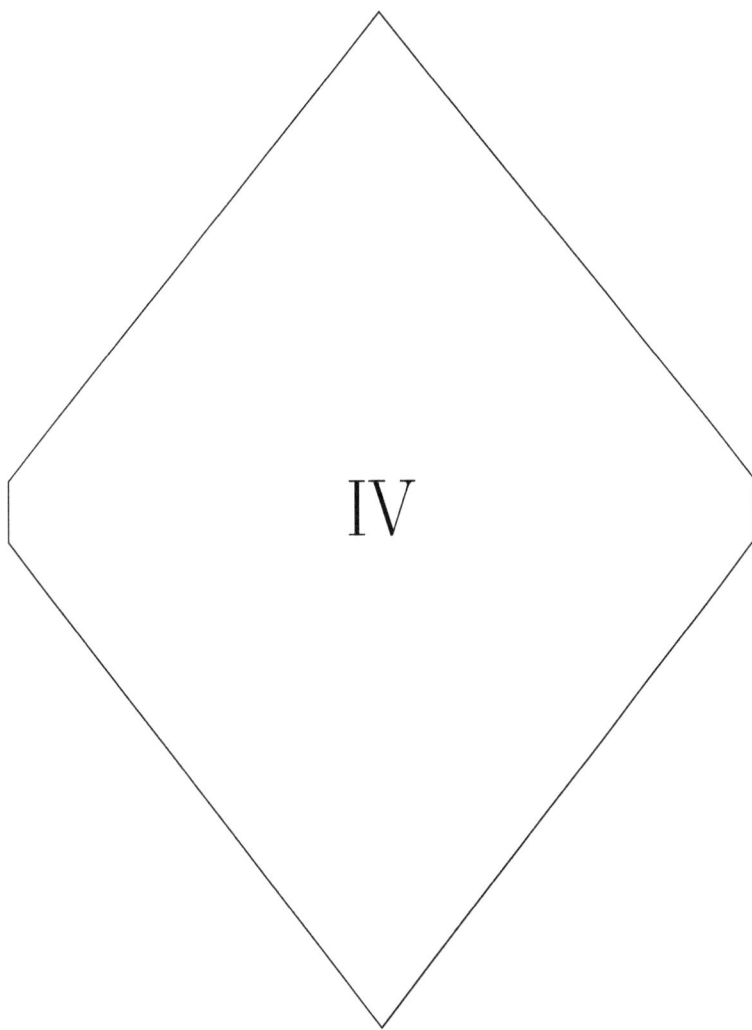

IV

New Figs

How long will it be before skin breaks
or anyone pays tribute to the fog?
How many gallons of mercury-
stained water does it take to float
a boat down the old Passaic
or to bathe the veins of a blue crab in the sun?
A man jumped at the Great Falls today.
The Palestinian barbershop was full.

We ran down the street to smell
the new figs at Nouri's,
not to taste them, but merely
to palm them between our knuckles,
test the mettle of their meat,
let the purple find dialogue with the bone.

Fern

Remnants of dead fern
stick to the screen
    a basement window.

Old wheelbarrow
abandoned to the snow.

    The late sun a liar
    in late winter.

Plastic

Ocean-dotted
green, yellow & white
with printing on it

we swim in it
holding a perfect crawl
like they taught us

back in tadpoles
when we were eleven
at Forsythe Pool

same as the sea turtle
the jellyfish
same as the dolphin and the whale

even the shorebirds
frolic in its waves and foam
mistaking it for the old nutrition

when oil was at home
in the rock

Notes on Progress

The great planes that flew at El Alamein
are thundering before takeoff
in a small backyard, either that
or the heavy-loaders are taking down
my former neighbor's house in the name
of progress and profit,
and maybe, in the name of God.

What is meant by the gods—another
quiet morning—a summer's morning with NPR
on the radio, and Sylvia Poggioli
reporting from Paris, her voice cracking open
spilling names in spite of higher windows
and big blue doors,
cinnamon molding around the floors.

Caught in the Binary (2)

Caught in the terrible binary,
bluecoat and Reb—

Mason, Dixon, wildwood
flower and raven hair

dry blood, brown dirt
plow blade and rust

making the cotton crop
then not making it—

In south Alabama, you breathe
salt without seeing water

grieve over an old rock
that marks a field hand's grave.

In Jersey, we cherish the gumption of February rain
its purple metallic odor

what's left of airplane
propellers and grenades.

Walter Benjamin crossed
the Pyrenees into Spain

with a satchel and a notebook,
a newspaper soiled by a rose

the sweat of hate bleeding
into his shoulders.

A sick man then, he
declared he'd seen enough

he knew the rest by the pain in his gut
—where the story bends

where suns gather their seed
and the scrub grass following.

Last Log

What makes a Hohenzollern or pike sweat a bucket in a pouring rain?

The life of Gavrilo Princip, I suspect, or another mirage,
one more blackened penny thrown to the flame.

When will the last monarch fall?

The day I stand in a neighbor's yard watching Mars
blitz the comets, painting syrup wagons red.

When will the last log on the bonfire break?

At daybreak, that's when, when we offer ourselves as driftwood
and squint into the dying oil lamp of the whale.

Cast your mind on other days
wrote Yeats
no doubt in a fog of Irish whisky dreaming

of some craggy shore on a day choked in October
color and our daughters weeping.

Legend of the Three Blakes

Blake was a printer like my father,
careful with his letters,
inks, palettes, and numbers,

working under the blue light
by the river, Blake by the Thames,
my father by the Ouachita.

They laughed then cried
over Jax beers at a low
place in the levee.

I was eleven, my sister
fourteen. It was the season of
catfish and bullfrogs,

night sounds of a grander
watery world, mosquitoes and
muddy toes.

We heard those evenings
below the moss banks
long before we saw them

amid the trot lines,
Vienna Sausage tins
and soggy cartons of Saltines,

before we heard voices
my father believed he heard
so many nights after the war,

voices luring him away from smells
of the Mudline, away from guinea hens
and milking cows, to back doors

and honky tonks, and finally
to the printing floor,
engraving tools, the 3 o'clock

whistle, sweating his undershirt,
taking the slow way across the river.

Caught in the Binary (3)

caught in the terrible binary
—skeleton and her skin

lamb's blood and
sawed bone in the trench at Verdun

screen-door Louisiana summer
a red-nosed Nor'easter baring its soul

my mother sewing a patch on my sleeve, gray sweater
hanging silent as the spring

Christmas Eve

Canister green, a few snowflakes
cookies you said that were baked by your
grandmother in Minsk.

We came to our senses then.
The death of sentiment—mortality
gushing through our veins.

Memorial Day, 2020

Amazing, how warm it is in the sun
how cold, how Atlantic cold
it is in the shade.

I've pulled up a blue blanket and wear it like a cape
like FDR at Yalta, sea air hitting his face
soothing his unsettled nerves.

Memorial Day, 1969

Brass players of the West Monroe High School marching band
march up DeSiard Street playing
"Stars and Stripes Forever,"

backs straight, holding their horns, holding their line against hell
and the backwaters of history
silver helmets glistening.

Marine's Diary

The luminaries were lit a night late
in the wherewithal of the pit of the stomach
old stone, the last of Christmas Eve
snow—wetness of our skin cooling
against the brief and the silent—

we hauled the high limbs from the Great Northern
Oak that was ambushed in the storm
and I remembered reading that Marine's
diary of World War II

about Okinawa and Peleliu
drift and rock and blood
and small, wiry boys who looked
toward the smear of one more ridge
for the slightest sign of God.

Haiku for Murakami

I want to die in
Hokkaido in winter when
seaweed is starved for love.

*

I want to die in
Hokkaido inside the winter
hush of the marsh.

Sundown, Orvieto

there is the aloneness of it,
old devil orange,

that burnt one of John Ford westerns
falling down on ancient stone,

failing spires of an ancient church,
the handsome mountain boy

waits my table, "spritz and chips,"
then again, his olive skin

gleaming in the twilight
like precious stone

me, suddenly alone
sipping my life from the wine.

Just Long Enough

My desire is only this—to die
someplace the earth made beautiful
all on its own,
the way a first-grader
makes the morning glory
out of construction paper
and Elmer's glue, or the way
the sun sets on Monument Valley.

I want to find my peace
with not too many people around,
a place no one else has found.
I want to be there just long
enough to recognize false light,
give it a name, something
out of Virgil, maybe, or Neruda.

Then set myself aside
like an old saddlebag
unafraid of the ground.

Leftover Cornbread

Martha Stewart's bay scallops
linger in my throat
like candles.

I can't get the sesame oil
out of my fingers, or spilled
ginger/vinegar

out of my nose
or the bottom
of the fridge.

Luckily there is rice,
leftover cornbread
my mother fed me in '62

with greased potatoes,
a side of hash
a spit of salt.

We took our supper
on the sun porch
with my sister
who was battling the lupus then
in the long hours on Mississippi Street.

Publication Credits

The following poems were published previously (in some cases in earlier versions) in these journals:

"Salvage," *Carve*

"Boyhood, Louisiana," and "Notes on Progress," *December*

"Choice," "Kudzu and Lime Plank," "Remind Me," "You Sing Softly," and "Sitting, Staring from a Bench at the Metropolitan Museum," *Exit 7*

"Six O'Clock on the Cape," *Juxtaprose*

"Leftover Fries" and "On an August Field," *Paterson Literary Review*

"Lacrosse at Memorial Field," *Exit 13*

"Sunny Day in Queens," *Pinyon Review*

"Iseult" and "French Cinema," *Platform Review*

"Caught in the Binary," and "Thoughts in a Blizzard," *Stillwater Review*

"The Day Mandela Died," *Terra Preta Review*

"Where Do the Gone Things Go," "Year of the Dragon," and "Dress Shop in Manaus," *U.S. 1 Worksheets*

"The Legend of the Three Blakes," "Minnieweather," and "Bayou," *Valley Voices*

"Tablets of Meaning" and "Tears for the Locust," *The Night Heron Barks*

A number of the poems appeared in the chapbook, *Boyhood, Louisiana,* selected as the poetry honoree in the *Platform Review Chapbook Series,* 2019. These include "Where Do the Gone Things Go," "Choice," "At a Newspaper Office...," Rialto Theater, 1964," "Caught in the Binary," "Six O'Clock on the Cape," "Alberta Seafood," "Sea Song," "Honey," "Thoughts in Winter," "Sundown, Orvieto," "Bayou," and "On an August Field."

In Appreciation

I wish to express sincerest gratitude to so many loving, encouraging friends, writers and poets who have placed their imprint on this collection:

Robert Lokey, Ted Haddin, Maria Mazziotti Gillan, and Andrea Gurwitt encouraged me to keep writing early and often to turn a love of poetry into art. All my teachers and friends from the Drew University MFA program inspired me to work and read and believe, and in their best moments dared me to stretch my bones. These include my mentors, Michael Waters, Judith Vollmer, Alicia Ostriker and Anne Marie Macari, as well as Mihaela Moscaliuc, Jane Mead, and Jean Valentine. Among my Drew peers who have remained loyal friends and constant sources of insight and strength, I owe particular thanks to Mary Brancaccio, Jesse Burns, David Crews, and Lynne McEniry.

Much gratitude goes out to Ellen Foos and Arlene Weiner at Ragged Sky Press—my capable editors who embraced this work and put elbow grease into it, and whose experience and instincts made it a more focused, tighter project than it might have been. And to artist Jean Foos, with whom I connected instantly, whose cover design and artistic vision seemed a natural, fitting fusion with the words on the page.

And to my sister, Sandra McGlothin, a bulwark of strength throughout my life, I cannot possibly say enough. Lastly, to Deborah, the spirit in my chest, who has stayed on this road with me so long, and who has often taken on the task, sometimes cheerfully, of being "first reader."

Bruce Lowry is a Louisiana native and "searcher," whose poetry, essays and journalism have been broadly recognized and honored. His writing has been shaped in part by his adolescence growing up in the Deep South of the 1960s and '70s, and has also been influenced by his parents' stories from their childhood in the sharecropper South of the Great Depression era. His poems, short stories and essays have been published widely. His poetry chapbook, "Boyhood, Louisiana" (Platform Review), was published in 2019. He has been thrice nominated for the Pushcart Prize and was twice awarded Honorable Mention for the Allen Ginsberg Prize. In 2014, he received an MFA in Poetry from Drew University, where his art came under the influence of numerous poets and mentors, including Michael Waters, Alicia Ostriker and Jean Valentine. His essay on the favelas of Rio de Janeiro, "Rio's Teeming Favelas Are a World Apart," written in 2001 during his time in Brazil as part of a Pew Journalism Fellowship, was anthologized and praised. In 2004, while working for the *Anniston Star* (Ala.), he earned Best Op-ed Feature Award from the National Association of Opinion Page Editors. In 2018, while Opinion Page Editor for the *Bergen Record* (N.J.), he was awarded first place for Editorial Writing by the New Jersey Press Association. He has taught literature, composition and history at the college level. He currently works as a senior communications associate in the State Legislature in Trenton, New Jersey, and continues to write both as an essayist and poet. Like Keats, Bashō and Tolstoy, he enjoys taking long walks to no place in particular. He lives with his partner and assorted cats in a 1950s house in Union County, New Jersey.

www.ingramcontent.com/pod-product-compliance
Lightning Source LLC
Chambersburg PA
CBHW031144090426
42738CB00008B/1221